FAMISHED!

52 Ingredients Your Body Is Really Starving For

Linda Bastian Barney

This book is dedicated to my husband, David –
my best friend, my rock, and the love of my life:

Thank you for giving me the courage to pursue all my wildest dreams

Ingredients

Acknowledgments

My heart is overflowing with love and appreciation for all of my family and friends who have been so supportive and who have cheered me on in the process of writing this book.

My deepest thanks to my soul mate, David, for your never ending support and devotion. I could not have done this without you.

To Michael, Corinne, and Lucie: Your love and support mean the world to me. Thank you for showing me how simply beautiful and sweet life can be.

To Jaron: I'm so thankful for your brilliant ideas and your fierce dedication to my work. I could not ask for a better personal assistant – you know exactly what my heart and soul are trying to express.

To Devin: You are my most enthusiastic fan and publicist. Thank you for always being there for every event and for bringing ten friends along with you for good measure. I hope to someday be as amazing as you tell everyone I am.

To Mom and Dad: Thank you for your examples of courage, love, hard work, and determination. Your adventurous spirits taught me how to fly.

To Debbie: Thanks for being the best "seester" in the world. You are always, always there for me, and I'm so grateful for your love.

To Lindsey Smith: Thank you for being so willing to share your expertise and for encouraging me to keep shining my light.

To Brandon Vanderstappen: I'm deeply grateful for our "pow-wow sessions" and all you have taught me over the years. You are a true and rare friend.

To David Calver: Thank you for so skillfully polishing and editing my manuscript without changing my voice. You are amazing!

To all other family, friends, and clients: Thank you from the bottom of my heart and soul for your love, kindness, and encouragement. I love connecting with each of you and being a part of your healing journeys. Wiz Khalinda out. ☺

Introduction

You stare into the refrigerator with a blank look on your face. You're hungry, starving, famished, but you don't know what for. There is an emptiness inside of you, and you want to fill it, but with what? Nothing looks good. Nothing sounds good. Nothing that is staring back at you from inside that refrigerator or pantry seems like it will satisfy you. So, are you really hungry, or is something else going on here? What are you REALLY starving for?

We've all had this experience at one time or another, so we can certainly all relate. It's a normal part of our human experience to feel hungry for something that we can't quite put our finger on – something other than the food that we eat. Part of our journey on this earth is learning how to respond to the hungers and desires that come with being alive.

Eating delicious foods that tantalize our taste buds is extremely satisfying and fun. And so it should be. Eating is one of our basic needs, right up there with sex, sleep and breathing. We should enjoy our food and savor it. That's how it was meant to be.

Food can make us feel loved, nurtured, and protected. Food can be an expression of creativity, a way to connect with friends and family, a reason to get up in the morning, and an event to look forward to with anticipation. For example, when you try out a new recipe and present it to your family, it can be extremely rewarding to watch them enjoy the flavors and ask for seconds. You have created something that your family loves, and that feels amazing! Or how about being super excited for Christmas so that you can enjoy the taste of your mom's famous English trifle and your sister's savory turkey stuffing - that's definitely something to look forward to!

But food can also give us a lot of grief. If we eat a food that we have designated as "off limits", we tend to feel guilty about it for days afterwards. For instance, we overindulge because that lasagna and garlic bread just tastes so darn good, and then we starve ourselves for the next 3 days to try and make up for it. There is a ton of emotion and neurosis tied up in what we eat, how much we eat, and when we eat it.

The fact of the matter is that we need food. We have to eat in order to keep on living. It should be one of the most enjoyable things about our lives, yet it can become a huge source of stress, worry, guilt, and misery. And why is that? It could be because we are giving food too much power. What I mean by that is we try to solve problems with food that have nothing to do with it. We feel lonely – we eat. We feel unappreciated – we eat. We feel misunderstood – we eat. We feel frustrated – we eat. Food seems like the quickest and easiest way to fill the void, because, well, it is. But covering up or masking our deepest desires and needs with a slice of cheesecake or a bowl of ice cream doesn't make those needs go away. They remain, only to resurface time and time again.

What if we decided to finally and fully pay attention to our bodies, what they really need, and what they really want? What would happen if we met those needs in a variety of ways, other than strictly with food? If we gave our bodies nourishment in the form of laughing with friends, walking in nature, creating beautiful artwork, writing a love song, or playing the most fun game ever - how would we feel then?

Let's take a look at some ways in which our bodies are famished – literally starving – and what we can give them so that they are completely nourished and functioning at the highest and best levels possible!

Ingredient #1:
Love

The number one missing ingredient that our bodies are starving for is love. The time we spend thinking about our bodies (if we think about them at all) is usually focused on what we dislike, hate, despise, and wish we could change about them. Most of us spend very little to no time focusing on what we love, appreciate, and are thankful for about our bodies right here, right now.

Our bodies love us so much that they are constantly sending us messages about what they need in order to function at their highest levels. These messages come in the form of moods, energy levels, cravings, pain, and sometimes even illness. When we listen to these messages and try to respond to them in a loving way, our bodies can heal and create a state of wellness.

Love accepts you just as you are, right now. Love says that no matter what you do, I will take care of you. Love says that I will be there for you. Love says that I will never hurt you. Love never criticizes, finds fault, nitpicks, or degrades. Love uplifts, praises, appreciates, and sees the beauty in all things. That's the kind of love our bodies crave. That's the kind of love our bodies deserve.

What is one loving thing that you can do for your body today?

Ingredient #2: Gratitude

When we are given a thoughtful, meaningful gift, what do we do? We say "thank you", don't we? We show appreciation, safeguard it, maybe even put it in a place of honor. Perhaps we think about how much work was required on the part of the giver in order to provide us with this wonderful gift, and we spend some time admiring this token of the giver's love for us. What we focus our gratitude on becomes even more beautiful, meaningful and special.

Your body is an amazing gift. Instead of taking it for granted, neglecting it, abusing it, or criticizing it for what it is not, try feeling grateful for it! What has your body already done for you today? Pumped blood to your heart and organs, breathed oxygen in and out of your lungs, digested the food you've eaten, eliminated toxins and waste, and regulated temperature, heart rate, hormone levels, and a thousand other systems, without you even having to think about it. That's something incredible to be thankful for.

Take some time to feel deep gratitude for the gift of your body. Show true appreciation for it in the way that you speak to and about it. Safeguard it by giving it fresh, wholesome foods and clean, pure water. Honor it by taking care of it in the very best ways you can think of. Spend some time admiring your body for all of its beautiful attributes. The things that we are most grateful for are the things that become our greatest treasures.

Feed your body gratitude, and watch it transform.

Ingredient #3:
Nutrition

It seems obvious, but I think that sometimes we forget to give our bodies the nutrition they really crave. We may grab a granola bar as we run out the door and call it breakfast, eat a cheeseburger and fries for lunch, and have a large helping of lasagna with breadsticks for dinner, but where is the real nutrition? Perhaps we throw a little bit of lettuce on the side, top it with ranch dressing and call it a salad, but since lettuce is mostly water, there's not much nutrition there either.

If we eat fake or processed food throughout the day, we will continue to feel hungry and dissatisfied. Our bodies crave the genuine nutrients that can only be found in real foods. By real foods, I mean foods that are still in or very close to their most natural state. The Standard American Diet (aka S.A.D.) consists mostly of highly processed, packaged, chemical-laden products that pose as food, but really aren't. We are so used to food being in little boxes or bags, that we don't even think about how long it has been in there, how it got there, or what had to happen to it in order to preserve it that way.

Our bodies are happy and healthy and can function at their best when we eat close to nature and close to home. When we eat a variety of fresh fruits, vegetables, herbs, grains, nuts, seeds and fats, we are giving our bodies wholesome fuel to run on. Try to eat as many colors of the rainbow in a day that you possibly can. Experiment with crazy-looking veggies you find at the farmer's market, or even try growing them in your own backyard. Aim to incorporate different textures, flavors, and sensations in every meal. Ditch the dead, packaged foods and switch to food that was recently alive. Make eating an adventure, and your body will come alive and thrive!

What is one way you can add more nutrition to your diet today?

Ingredient #4:
Sweetness

I'm not talking about the sugary sweetness of a cupcake, donut or candy bar. I'm not even referring to those marshmallow puffs covered with bright pink sugar. The sweetness our bodies are really hungry for is the kind that doesn't come in a package. Real sweetness is more than just a temporary sugar rush; it's a lasting feeling of giving and receiving love, tenderness, and sincerity.

If we only look for it, there is an abundance of sweetness in life to fill us up. Think of how sweet it is when a little child wraps their arms around your neck and squeezes you oh so tightly. Remember the delight and thrill you felt when you said, "I love you" for the first time. Imagine the pleasure of a first kiss or the lingering embrace of a long-absent loved one. Our bodies crave those sweet moments of connection with the people that we love. When we don't get enough of that kind of sweetness, we tend to turn to sugary sweets to try to fill the void.

We can add more sweetness to our daily lives by hugging more, giving more kisses, and being generous with words of kindness and love.

Maybe you feel like you're not a hugger, but who's to say that you can't become one? Try hugging lots of people, and just see how it goes. My guess is that you will love it, and since most people enjoy being hugged, those you wrap your arms around will love it too! Give compliments, say "I love you" often to family and friends, and smother your children and spouse with kisses galore.

The more sweetness you bring into your life by being more open and affectionate, the less you will need those fluffy, pink, sugar-coated domes in order to feel satisfied.

Life is sweet. Savor it!

Ingredient #5:
Movement

Our bodies were made for moving. As soon as a newborn baby is able, they start trying to move. Their arms and legs are continuously kicking and waving. Soon they start rolling over, crawling, walking, and eventually running. It is in our nature to crave movement, to want to explore our environment. But as we get older, we can tend to move around less and less. Perhaps we sit at a desk for a good portion of the day, and then when we get home, we are so tired that we plop down on the sofa and that's it. We're done. This is a natural inclination, but one we could perhaps be more mindful of.

Getting out in the fresh air and going for a walk is a great way to boost your energy levels. You may think you're too tired to do so, but once you get out there and get going, your energy will increase. The oxygen outside in nature is much more energizing than the air in your living room or even inside a gym. Take every opportunity to get out and explore the world around you. There is so much beauty just outside your door, and it's waiting for you to go and find it!

So take a hike, go for a swim, run a lap, do yoga on the beach, build a snowman, hunt for cool rocks, or toss a ball around. Do whatever you find enjoyable that gives your body the movement it craves. Life is too short to spend it couch surfing. Maybe some actual surfing is what would really make your body feel happy and energized today!

How can you give your body the movement it is craving right now? Put this book down and go do it!

Ingredient #6:
Spirituality

Have you ever been to a funeral? If you have, then you have probably seen a body in a casket and you know that the person who once inhabited that body is no longer in there. Each of our bodies is powered by our spirit, and when that spirit leaves, the body is merely a shell, an empty pod where the spirit once resided. But while we are living, the spirit and the body are intertwined, connected, and inseparable.

Because of this profound relationship with our spirits, our bodies crave connection with a higher power, the source of our creation. We long to feel a part of something greater than ourselves, and to realize that our existence has some meaning in the grand scheme of things. Without this spiritual connection, we may feel depressed, lethargic, sad, or even hopeless. The body functions and feels its best when it receives a regular dose of meaningful spirituality. Developing a daily spiritual practice can be a powerful way to create a state of wellness in the body.

A spiritual practice can be anything that helps you feel calm, connected to your higher power, or at one with the universe. Some may enjoy prayer or meditation. Others may gravitate towards spending time in nature, listening to music, or reading inspiring books or scripture. Find whatever works for you, and do it every single day. Make it a non-negotiable part of your day that you can count on with anticipation. That daily dose of respite from the world will bring an added measure of health that your body will thank you for.

Begin or deepen your daily spiritual practice today, and start reaping the benefits to your body, mind, and soul!

Ingredient #7:
Stillness

In addition to regular movement, our bodies also need regular stillness. I am not referring to the stillness we experience while sleeping, vegging out in front of the TV, or taking an afternoon nap. I'm talking about a more active stillness – one in which we are fully awake and participating in being still.

Life gives us plenty of opportunities to practice stillness. How many times a day are we stuck in traffic, placed on hold, or told to "have a seat and we'll be right with you"? These moments are opportunities to practice being still, or, in other words, to practice "being". These moments in between the events of our day are a great time to be still, breathe, and renew our sense of self. A moment of peace and tranquility in the middle of a hectic day can be just the nourishment we need.

Commonly, our reaction to having to wait our turn or pause temporarily from whatever we're doing is to become impatient, honk our horn, turn on some music, or drum our fingers nervously. Why is being still so hard? I think it's because the mind likes having a task, something to keep it occupied. When we are left alone with our thoughts, we may be forced to confront our fears, think about ourselves, or face our demons. The mind will go to great lengths to avoid such daunting tasks.

The next time you are stuck in traffic, turn off the radio, clear your mind, and take a few deep breaths. Allow your body and mind to be fully in the present moment and accept it as it comes. Let go of any thoughts of the past ("Why would he say that to me?") as well as any thoughts of the future ("How am I going to get everything done?"). Being still and being in the moment will bring you back to yourself, back to reality, and back to an appreciation for the beauty of life.

Every single moment can be simply amazing if you just let go, breathe, and be.

Ingredient #8: Creativity

All of life is in a constant state of creation. Our very bodies are continuously recreating themselves. Our skin, bones, muscles, organs, blood, hair, and tissues are always regenerating, renewing themselves. Creativity is life, and life is creativity. And so it makes sense that our minds and bodies crave the notion of bringing something new into existence. It's what reminds us that we are alive, that life is exciting, and that something unique is just around the corner.

As children, we were bold creators. We lived in a world of imagination and endless possibilities. Life was a game filled with dragons, magic, mermaids, and journeys to faraway lands. Monsters could live in our closets and Santa Claus could fit down our chimney. But as we grew older and the seriousness of life began to weigh upon us, we had less and less time for fantasy, play, and make-believe. Somewhere along the way, we lost our creative, spontaneous, playful selves and became the dreaded "grown-ups". Where did our creativity go?

Being creative means different things to different people. For one person it may be composing music or painting a portrait. For another it may mean cultivating a beautiful garden or decorating a room. The possibilities are as numberless as the amount of people on the earth. Each of us is endowed with a creative gift - the ability to bring forth a part of ourselves to share with the world. When we honor that creative force inside of us, we are allowing ourselves to come alive, to really experience life on the highest level.

Whether you write a book, invent a gadget, or bake a fabulous cake, do something that stimulates your creativity on a regular basis. The satisfaction you feel will be worth the effort, and you will find joy in the process of creating an original gift from the heart.

What does your inner creative child want to do today? Go do it!

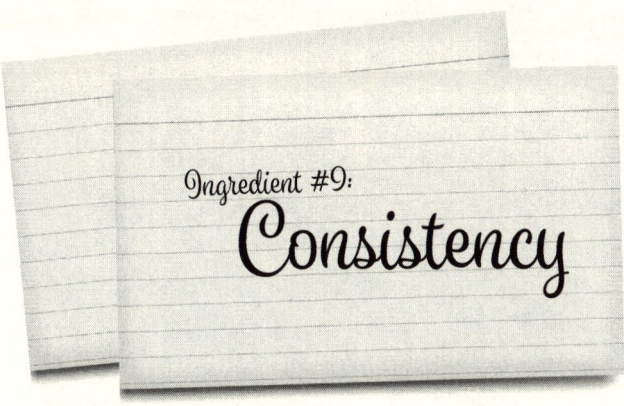

Ingredient #9:

Consistency

There's something to be said for having a routine. At first glance, it may seem a little boring to repeat the same pattern day after day, but if you go a little deeper, you will see the wisdom of it. Small children crave the safety of knowing that certain activities will occur at the same time each day. For the older generation, having a set schedule can bring a feeling of comfort and stability. So, it is perfectly reasonable that our bodies would crave consistency and regularity as well.

One way you can give your body more consistency is to automate your eating. It's okay to eat the same thing for breakfast every morning, or most mornings. It's even okay to eat basically the same thing for lunch on a daily basis. Just find something healthy and simple that you know you like, then go ahead and enjoy it on the daily! For example, I have bran toast topped with coconut oil, fresh berries, and a green drink for breakfast every morning. Lunch is usually leafy greens topped with lots of veggies and chicken. My body responds well to these foods and feels great when I eat them.

Automating my food in this way removes the pressure of having to decide what to prepare and eat for each meal. For two out of three of my daily meals, I already know what I'll be eating, and it's one less thing I have to worry about. The variety comes at dinnertime when I incorporate new recipes alongside old favorites, adding in lots of colors, textures, and flavors. Having this consistency helps my body to function at the highest levels possible, and keeps my digestive system from getting out of whack.

How can you automate your eating? Find a food that makes you feel amazing when you eat it, and see if you like eating it every day. Keep experimenting until you find a routine that works for you!

Ingredient #10:
Laughter

When was the last time you laughed really hard? I'm talking about a good, deep belly laugh that made your eyes water and your face hurt. If you haven't laughed that hard in a while, perhaps it's time to lighten up. Laughter can relieve stress, calm our nerves, improve our mood and help us relax. Laughing can make us feel good in a way that nothing else can. Sharing a laugh with friends or family is one of the most enjoyable ways we can improve our health.

When we laugh our bodies release endorphins, hormones that act as natural painkillers. This is why we literally feel better after a good laugh. Studies show that laughter reduces blood pressure, boosts immunity, eases chronic pain, improves heart health, and promotes an overall sense of well-being. If you laugh long and hard enough, you can even give your abs a good workout!

Sometimes as adults we forget how to have fun. Life can be busy, demanding and stressful, and we may feel like there's not enough time for silliness. If hearing other people laughing and having fun annoys you, it's a good bet that you haven't laughed, really laughed, in quite a while. Maybe it's time you did. Go see a silly movie, go out to a comedy club, or call up that old friend who can always make you laugh so hard that you almost pee your pants. Having a good, long laughing session is more cathartic than having a good cry, and your sinuses won't hurt when you're done.

Look on the bright side of life, step back and see how funny it really is, then go ahead and LOL!

Ingredient #11:
Water

Most of us are walking around dehydrated and we don't even know it. If you wait until you feel thirsty to take a drink, it's already too late. Feeling thirsty is one of the last signs of dehydration. Our bodies are mostly made up of water, so it makes sense that we need to replenish that supply often in order to keep our bodies functioning at optimal levels.

Getting a sufficient intake of water helps our bodies to break down food more effectively, overcome sugar and salt cravings, eliminate pain, lower blood pressure, and lose excess weight. Without enough water, our bodies will quickly begin to shut down and cease to function. Symptoms such as fatigue, headache, impaired judgment, decreased urine output, dark yellow or orange urine, and dry skin, nose and mouth are among the first indications that the body is in need of water.

A good rule of thumb is to drink at least half of your body weight in ounces every day. So if you weigh 150 pounds, you need to drink at least 75 ounces of water daily. This may seem like a lot at first, but you will soon get used to it, and actually you'll soon wonder how you ever survived without it. Buy yourself a cute refillable cup that you can carry with you wherever you go. Never leave the house without your water cup. Some people fill up a gallon jug and carry it with them throughout the day. Personally, I prefer to refill my cup with ice water throughout the day, but do whatever works best for you. Adding some fresh fruit or mint leaves to your water can give it some flavor and make it more enjoyable if you have a hard time at first.

A great book to read on this subject is "Your Body's Many Cries for Water" by F. Batmanghelidj, M.D. You'll be amazed at all the health benefits you can enjoy by doing this one simple thing. Make friends with water. Always have water with you wherever you go. Put it next to your cell phone, and never leave home without it.

Ingredient #12:
Chewing

Most of us don't take the time to chew our food properly. Usually, we are scoffing something down before we dash out of the house to the next activity, or we eat on the go in our cars or between meetings at the office. In our fast-paced society, we rarely take time to slow down and pay attention to the food that's in front of us.

The digestion process actually begins in the mouth. It starts with the production of saliva when we smell food cooking or sit down to a meal. The act of chewing triggers more saliva production, which helps break down the food and release the nutrients it contains. If we are not chewing enough times before we swallow, the stomach will have to work harder to digest the food, and we may end up with gas, bloating, heartburn, or other intestinal issues.

A good experiment is to try chewing each bite of food you take 30, 40, or even 50 times before swallowing. This forces you to slow down, really taste your food, and think about what you're eating. Try eating in a quiet room - no TV, no internet, no phone. Just concentrate on your meal, how it's nourishing your body, and how it smells, looks, feels, and tastes. You'll be amazed at how much better you feel after eating a meal this way, because you will be making the digestion process much easier for your body to handle.

Another fun activity is what I call the Chocolate Meditation. Buy some very high-quality chocolate, preferably something that comes individually wrapped, and eat it in much the same way as the chewing experiment. Unwrap the chocolate slowly. Notice the sound the wrapper makes. What does it smell like? How does it feel in your hand? Place the chocolate on your tongue and leave it there for a moment. Notice the sensation as it begins to melt in your mouth. What flavors and notes do you notice first? Can you taste vanilla, cinnamon, or other flavors you haven't noticed before? Take your time and really savor each and every bite like you have never tasted chocolate before. This is a simple way to train your body to slow down, taste your food, and prepare to be nourished.

Remember this mantra: The more you chew, the less work your stomach will have to do!

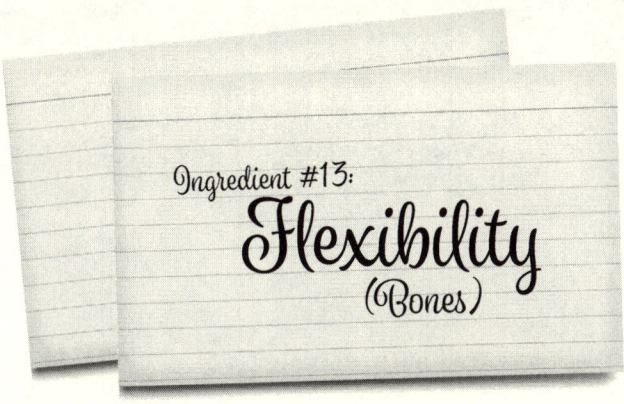

Ingredient #13:
Flexibility
(Bones)

To be flexible is to be "capable of being bent, usually without break-ing" (dictionary.reference.com). Since we are designed for movement, it makes sense that flexibility is an important ingredient our bodies need. We hear a lot about having strong bones, but in order to resist breaking, our bones also need to be flexible.

To keep your bones flexible and less prone to breakage, make sure you get plenty of bone broth. Bone broth contains lots of collagen, calcium, magnesium, glucosamine, and other nutrients that help keep our bones strong and pliable. Avoid overusing chewable antacids – these can con-tribute to brittle bones, constipation, acid reflux, kidney stones and other kidney related problems.

Make a simple bone broth by seasoning and cooking a whole, organic chicken, bones and all, on low in a slow cooker for about 4 hours. Remove the meat from the bones and set aside for later use. Add 2 tbsp. of apple cider vinegar to the pot, and continue to cook the bones in the liquid for another 12-20 hours. Remove any scum that rises to the top. Use the broth to make soup or for use in other recipes. Bone broth can also be made with bone in cuts of beef, pork, and even fish.

Make the choice to protect and care for your bones and keep them flexible and strong.

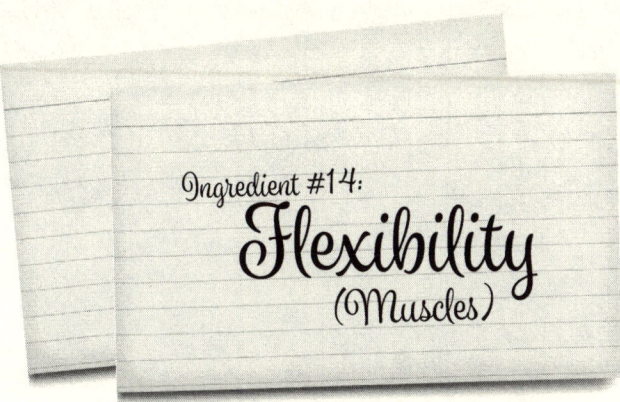

Ingredient #14:
Flexibility
(Muscles)

Yoga, Pilates, or some basic stretching exercises will go a long way in helping to keep your muscles flexible. Our bodies tend to get more stiff and rigid with time, and if we aren't making an effort to keep our muscles and joints in good working order, we could suffer the consequences later in life. A good rule of thumb is to spend at least 20 minutes each day stretching, as well as remembering to stretch periodically throughout the day if you sit a lot or work at a desk.

If you feel like your day is already jam packed and you have no time, stretch while you watch the news for 20 minutes or during your favorite 30-minute sitcom. Find a way to work your yoga or stretching routine into something you are already doing every day. That way, no extra time is required, and you have a trigger set up to remind you to do it.

When our muscles are strong, flexible, and healthy, we're less likely to suffer muscle tears and spasms, osteoporosis, muscle and joint pain, fatigue, inflammation and injuries. No one wants to be old, tired, and stiff as a board! You're only as young as you are flexible, so be sure to give your muscles some love in the form of stretching and movement every day.

Remember to do some warm-up stretches before going walking, running, or playing sports of any kind. This will help prevent injuries during the activity and muscle soreness the next day. Drinking plenty of water after a workout will also help keep your muscles flexible and healthy!

Keeping our muscles limber is vital to our health as we age, and every one of us is aging a little bit every day!

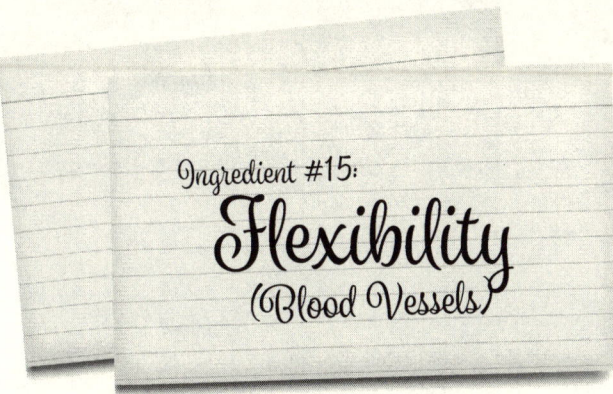

Ingredient #15:
Flexibility
(Blood Vessels)

We want our veins and arteries to remain flexible and open as we age in order to prevent high blood pressure and atherosclerosis, otherwise known as hardening of the arteries. A good way to keep our circulatory systems running smoothly and in top condition is through our diet. Healthy Omega 3 fats are vital to the health of our heart, arteries, veins, and blood vessels. Some good Omega 3 fats to start including in your diet are olive oil, coconut oil, fish oil, nuts and seeds.

Cooking: Switch from vegetable oil to an organic extra virgin olive oil for sautéing vegetables. Use organic coconut oil to pop popcorn instead of the fake butter flavored stuff. Spread coconut oil on your toast in the morning instead of butter. Experiment with using different oils for different recipes depending on what flavor you want to bring out in the dish.

Supplements: Get at least 1000 milligrams of a good-quality fish or krill oil every day. You can get them in liquid form as well as in capsules. Most high-quality fish oils will not leave you with a fishy aftertaste and will not cause burping or gas. If you do experience a mild fishy taste or burping, try taking your supplements in the middle of your meal for easier diges-tion. I take mine every morning about halfway through my breakfast.

Beauty: Experts recommend getting at least 2 to 3 tablespoons of coco-nut oil into your body each day in order to experience the maximum benefits. However, it can be hard to get that amount through diet alone. The skin, our largest organ, can also absorb the nutrients found in coco-nut oil when we apply it topically. I have found that it works extremely well as a facial moisturizer, a make-up remover, and as a body moisturizer too.

Switch out your creams, lotions, and cleansers with an organic, food-grade coconut oil, and I promise you, your skin, hair, nails and heart will thank you!

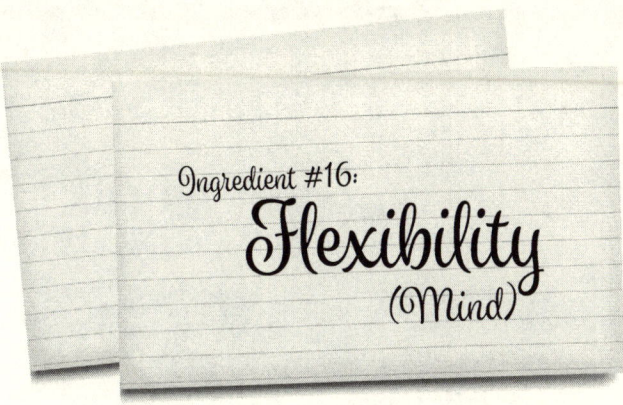

Ingredient #16:
Flexibility
(Mind)

We all probably know someone who is stiff, rigid, and set in their ways. How much fun is that person to be around? They go on and on about the same old problems, never want to try anything new, and never want to explore new ideas or concepts. They always eat at the same restaurants, order the same thing off the menu, watch the same types of movies, and shop at the same stores. Yes, life is predictable for these types of people, and that probably makes them feel safe on some level. But at the end of the day, never trying anything new only leads to disappointment and regret.

Our bodies do crave a routine, but they also crave new and exciting adventures. As good as it is to have a schedule, know your routine and have a plan, it is just as good to branch out once in a while and try something new! Do you only like reading one type of book? Why not pick up a totally new genre that you've never considered reading before? You may find that a new love develops for this previously unexplored territory.

Maybe you prefer watching movies, and hardly ever think about reading. Or maybe you feel like you just don't have time to read. As a lover of books, I can tell you that taking the time to read will only add to your enjoyment of and zest for life. Now might be a good time to step out of that comfort zone on your sofa, head over to the local bookstore, and purchase your first book in years.

Part of having a flexible mind is being open to new ideas. Just because something has always been a certain way doesn't mean that it should remain the same always and forever. Times change. People change. Ideas change. Be willing to consider that maybe, just maybe, you have been hanging on a bit too long to some old, outdated ways of thinking or being, and allow yourself to evolve.

It may be that the more resistance we feel to change, the more urgent it is to be willing to change.

Ingredient #17:
Optimism

Half of adult Americans consider themselves optimists, according to a 2013 survey (http://www.statista.com/statistics/262675/survey-on-optimism-or-pessimism/). But what about the other 50 percent of us? Do we tend to see the glass as half empty? Do we expect the worst to happen instead of the best? Are we always on the lookout for those who may try to take advantage, mislead, or hurt us? Having a pessimistic view of life can take its toll on us emotionally, spiritually, and physically. Our bodies are starving for more optimism, more anticipation of happy endings, and higher expectations.

Think about it - if you expect your body to get weak, fat, tired, and run-down as you age, then those things will more than likely transpire. If you expect people to hurt you, take you for granted, use you and abuse you, then as a general rule, they probably will. If you give up hope of answered prayers, dreams coming true, and magical events transpiring, then by and large, none of those things will happen either. For the most part, we get what we expect to get in life – no more, no less.

What if those of us who are among the 50% who see the glass as half empty started to believe only the best about ourselves, others, and life in general? What would happen if we simply decided to think about all of the good things that could happen instead of focusing on the worst-case scenario? What if we expected wonderful, beautiful, magical events to transpire when we woke up in the morning? What if we could foresee our bodies growing healthier, stronger, and more full of life and energy on a daily basis? What changes would come to pass? How much happier would we be?

I believe that a huge shift in our collective consciousness would take place if we could all be a little more positive in our thinking. Let's start today by replacing negative, self-defeating thoughts with positive, uplifting, hopeful thoughts and attitudes. When a negative thought pops in for a visit, simply replace it with a positive one.

Just for today, expect great things to happen. And they will.

Ingredient #18:
Expression

I remember seeing a video once on social media of a man dancing through the streets of New York City. He had on his headphones, and while listening to his iPod, he grooved his way around town, bringing smiles to the faces of surprised onlookers. He had no particular agenda or message, he just felt like dancing. So he did.

Most of us have had a time when we were so full of life, love, and joy that we felt like dancing in the streets too. But we probably didn't. It isn't considered proper to dance around like a fool in public. People might stare at us, laugh at us, ridicule us, or perhaps even make a rude comment. Or would they? When people in New York saw the dancing man, most of them smiled, laughed with enjoyment, and went about their day. Some of them even commented that they wished they were brave enough to do what he was doing. He was expressing his joy the best way he knew how. He felt like dancing, and so he danced.

Our emotions, whether positive or negative, often go unexpressed out of fear of looking foolish. How often do we fight back tears because we don't want our makeup to run, our eyes to turn red, and our face to get all blotchy? How many times do we want to give someone a giant hug, but settle for a handshake instead? It may feel safer to keep our joy, our sadness and our hearts hidden away, but when we do, we miss out on a lot. This is real life. We don't get a do over. Right here and right now is all we have, and if we don't fully immerse ourselves in life's events, we will have missed the point.

Practice letting go of fears, inhibitions, and propriety by openly and honestly expressing yourself. You may find that life is more enjoyable that way. It may get a little messy at times, but at least at the end of the day you'll know you spoke your truth, conveyed your feelings, and shared the love in your heart.

Ingredient #19:
Adventure

I am writing this on what would have been my dad's 86th birthday. He died over 12 years ago of Parkinson's disease at age 74. As I woke up this morning, my first thoughts were of him – of how much he loved life, his dedication to his family, his sense of humor, his laugh. My dad knew how to make life an adventure, and life was never dull when he was around. He was always passionate about what he was doing, whether he was hiking off into the wilderness, roping a cow, riding a horse, or just sitting down with a cup of coffee. My dad did everything with gusto.

Many of us lead predictable, and you could even say boring, lives. We don't take too many chances, we resist change, and we stick to what is familiar. But in order to feel alive, really alive, our bodies need a sense of adventure. We need to feel the wind in our face once in a while, we need to risk looking or feeling a little silly, we need to take a leap of faith. If all we ever do is stand on the sidelines, watching everyone else playing the game but never joining in ourselves, we will live to regret it later on.

Someone once said that there is no growth in the comfort zone, and no comfort in the growth zone. Our bodies, minds, and souls are yearning to grow and stretch beyond their current limits. That's why we're here, after all. But in order to grow and progress, we have to step outside of our comfort zones now and then, take a chance, and try something different. We need to develop a sense of adventure about life. Playing it safe may feel like the right thing to do, but in the end, when we look back, we will remember the huge leaps of faith as our moments of greatest growth and achievement.

My dad was a great example of someone who lived life on his terms, took chances, made mistakes, then got back up and tried it all again. Who do you know that lives an adventurous, daring, exciting life? Channel some inspiration from them, take that first step into the growth zone, and then go out and really live!

Ingredient #20:
Prayer

I was on a beach in Hawaii with my husband, my sister, and my brother in law a few years ago, when we were approached by a rather rough-looking dude. He wanted to know one thing from us: "Do you fear God?" His question was unexpected, and quite frankly a little disturbing. Who was this stranger to ask me such a deep and penetrating question as this? We had a long and sometimes animated conversation with him, in which he told us that he knew God did not exist because He had not answered his specific prayers. No matter what we said, we could not convince him that prayer is a little more complicated than that. He eventually left us, and set out to share his story of disillusionment with other beachgoers.

What I realized from talking with this man is that prayer is not a phone that we can pick up, dial in, and put in our order for what we think we need that day. As tempting as it may be to tell God what we need, He already knows. And usually, what we think we need or want is not at all what God has in mind for us.

Prayer is a reminder. It is a way for us to remember all the goodness that we've received in the past, and that we will yet receive. It's an acknowledgement that we are not in control, no matter how much we would like to believe that we are. Prayer is an expression of faith that everything will be okay, that we will be okay, even if we are temporarily lost, disillusioned, angry, hurt, or afraid. The act of saying a prayer, whether vocalized or just felt in our hearts, is a way of holding on when all we really want to do is let go.

Our bodies want and need to pray, to feel connected to a higher source, to be relieved of our burdens if only for a few moments. From a prayer offered on bended knees with arms folded, to a thought or feeling of gratitude held in meditation, to a whispered "thank you", all forms of prayer bring us back to awareness of our fragility. When we connect with God in prayer, life is a little easier to bear, the future is more hopeful, and our hearts and minds are a little bit lighter.

How do you pray? Forget about what it might look like to anyone else, and pray in the way that feels right to you.

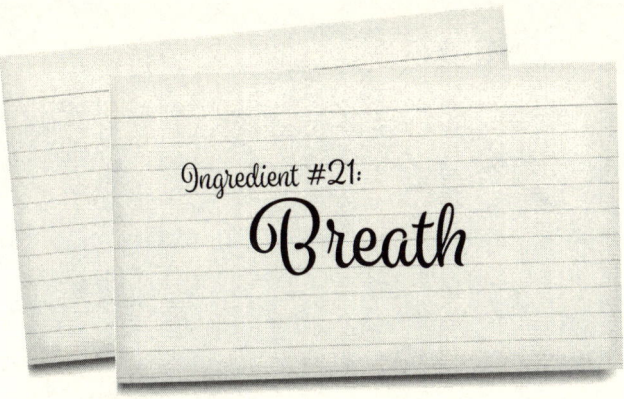

Ingredient #21:
Breath

Breathing is so vital to life that we can't go more than a few seconds without it. Breath is literally life. Yet so often, we neglect to think about how important our breath is to our wellbeing. How often are we concentrating so hard and trying so diligently that we just forget to breathe? I know I have caught myself on several occasions just holding my breath and waiting for the moment or pain to pass.

When we hold our breath, we are stopping, or at least attempting to stop, whatever is happening. When we let go and just breathe, we are allowing and making space for life to unfold. We run around making things happen all day long, but how often do we just sit down, take in a deep breath, and relax into the moment? How many times a day would a good cleansing breath help us become more focused, more aware, and more at ease?

For many years, I felt like I had to earn my existence on this earth. I thought I should always be busy, have a million and one things to do, take care of everyone and everything, never stopping or slowing down. But years of panic attacks, anxiety, and stress related health problems eventually proved to me that I was dead wrong. My worth does not depend on how busy I am, or how many tasks I can accomplish in a day. I am worth something even if I don't get one single thing done today. It took me a long time to figure that out.

You are of value because you exist. You are here. You are alive. You are breathing in and out. And even if that were all you were able to do for the rest of your life, just breathe in and out, you would still be of infinite worth and value. It's good to have goals, dreams, aspirations, and plans. It's also good to have time to stop, listen, think, and breathe. Life is a journey, not a race. Whether we arrive at our final destination panting and out of breath or in a calm, relaxed state of mind is entirely up to us.

Take a deep breath. Hold it for a few seconds. Now let it out. Do that a few more times. Close your eyes and feel the breath entering and exiting your body. Relax. Breathe. You deserve it.

Ingredient #22:
Connection

How thrilling is it when you meet someone who is from the same hometown as you? How excited do you get when you hear the person next to you at a party saying how much they love a restaurant that just happens to be your favorite too? Why is it so important to us to have a hometown, a favorite restaurant, a hobby or just anything in common with someone else? Why does it feel so good to say, "Oh my gosh, me too!"? It's because we all crave connection.

It's part of the human existence to feel isolated, alone, and solitary at times – to feel that no one else really understands you, knows you, or "gets" you. That part of our brain that Sigmund Freud referred to as the Ego loves to make us feel like we are so unique, so rare and so different from everyone else that nobody but us could ever understand it. Countless songs and poems have been written alluding to this facet of the human psyche.

I am in no way saying that you're not special or unique, because you absolutely are! In fact, I once saw a drink coaster that summed it up perfectly: "You are unique. Just like everyone else." The truth is that you are fabulously unique. You're one of a kind. There is no one else out there exactly like you. But this doesn't mean that you are somehow disconnected or set apart from the rest of the world. On the contrary, we are all very much connected to and intertwined with one another.

When the Twin Towers fell on 9/11, we came together as a nation and acknowledged our connection to our fellow citizens. I remember walking through a store that day and being able to palpably feel the weight of our collective grief. The people in those buildings, none of whom I knew personally, were my brothers, my sisters, my family members. They were me.

It's true that one part of us feels isolated and separate from the rest of the world. But there's another, stronger part that knows, with the deep knowing that comes from our very soul, that we are all connected. What affects one affects us all. It's painful at times to have our hearts so interwoven, but it's worth it. It's what makes us uniquely human.

Ingredient #23:
Grounding

When was the last time you walked outside in your bare feet? Can you remember how it felt? Maybe it was on a beach where the warm, soft sand squished up between your toes. Maybe it was in a garden where the dark, rich soil felt cold and moist against your skin. No matter where it was, you probably remember feeling calm, peaceful, and content in that moment. That's because there's a connection between our bodies and the earth.

We are electrical beings living on an electrical planet. All matter has a vibration, including humans. It just so happens that our vibration, or dominant oscillatory rate, matches up perfectly with that of the earth. So when we step outside of our homes, our office cubicles, our cars, and our shoes, and really get connected to Mother Earth, we start to feel better almost immediately! Think about how much more at ease, how much happier, and how much more relaxed you feel when you are standing next to a waterfall rather than next to a computer. Nature has a unique power to bring our vibration into harmony with its own vibration. All it takes is a little of our time and some fresh air.

Grounding has become a trendy thing to do in recent years. You can buy a grounding mat to put your feet on while working at your desk, a grounding sheet to sleep on, and grounding shoes to keep you connected to the earth. But I believe the best, most natural and least expensive way to get grounded is to actually go outside. Take a few minutes each day to step out into nature and commune with her. Maybe you could start a herb garden on your patio, plant some tomatoes and peppers in your backyard, or buy a colorful pot and fill it with a variety of beautiful flowers. Or maybe you just want to take off your socks and shoes and sit on the grass for a few minutes each day.

Our bodies need to feel connected to the earth. If we give ourselves permission to slow down, step outside, and enjoy being in nature for short while, we will reap the benefits in a big way. The healing energy of the earth will help us sleep better, feel healthier, and live happier. And it's as simple and accessible as the ground beneath our feet.

Ingredient #24:
Space

Recently I have felt the need to get rid of clutter in my closets, drawers, cabinets, pantry, and my entire house and life. I am not a hoarder by any means; in fact, I'm quite the opposite. I love the feeling of getting rid of items that have outlived their purpose. But even so, stuff just seems to pile up around us when we aren't looking. It just happens. Even to non-hoarders like me.

I had been reading a lot about a minimalist lifestyle, and in particular, minimalist wardrobes. This intrigued me. I wondered how I would get by with only a limited number of clothing items to choose from. Would it simplify my life, or end up making me feel frustrated and sad? (Just so you know, I long ago kicked my husband out of our walk-in closet and delegated his clothes to the bedroom closet across the hall.) So, as an experiment, I removed about 75% of my wardrobe items and stashed them away in my basement (just in case). And for the past 5 months I have been "making do" with only 25% of what I actually own. What was the result? Truthfully, I love it!

Famished!

Not having an overwhelming amount of clothing items to choose from when I get dressed has made my mornings much more enjoyable. Paring down my choices to a few basic items, in a few basic colors, has been incredibly liberating! I also simplified my small kitchen by removing all the extra dishes, cooking gadgets, mugs, and utensils that had accumulated over the years. Now I can actually see what I have and the essentials are easily accessible. It's incredible. Life changing, in fact.

Our bodies need to have some space, some room to breathe. If our closets, drawers, and homes are full to capacity, it can begin to feel suffocating. Keeping life simple, being content with what we have, and realizing that what we already have is enough is truly a source of joy and peace.

Is there an area of your home that you can clear out and create some space in? Try donating some of your excess goods to charity, or give them to a family member or friend, and see how much lighter it makes you feel!

Ingredient #25:
Light

For the past week or so, the valley where I live has been stuck in an inversion. As happens occasionally in the winter, pollution and cold, stagnant air combine to create this miserable weather pattern. Thick, grey clouds of smog and haze cover the sun and sky, making it seem as though we're living in a giant smoke chamber. The weatherman reports that it will be another 8 days before a storm moves in and clears the air. And I want to punch him in the face.

When we are deprived of sunlight, our bodies and minds become lethargic, listless, depressed or in severe cases, even suicidal. Humans are beings of light. We emit light, we absorb light, and we are created, at least in part, from light. As such, it's only natural that we crave the warmth and energy that comes from the largest power source in the solar system. Think of it this way - if you plant a flower in the richest soil, water it, fertilize it, and then place it in a dark room, it will wither and die. The same is true for us. We may have the most nutritious foods to eat, plenty of clean, fresh water to drink, and the most comfortable living conditions – but without light, we will still struggle to survive.

My solution to the haze problem in our valley was to take a short drive up the canyon. As soon as I left the valley and rose above the inversion, blue skies and sunshine emerged, and I immediately felt better. My mood improved, my mind was clear, and I could breathe again. The power and wisdom of Mother Nature never cease to amaze me!

Make an effort to bring light into your life every single day. If you work indoors, you may want to consider investing in a light box or taking a short walk outside on your lunch break. Plan outdoor activities on weekends. Dine al fresco as often as you can. Open up the blinds and curtains in your home and let the sunshine in. Remember, light is our friend, and it's also an essential component to being happy, healthy, and sane.

Ingredient #26:
Darkness

This past summer I went on a 10-day fishing trip to Alaska with my family. The scenery was spectacular, the air was crisp and refreshing, and the fishing was exceptional. There was just one problem – it never got dark. Because of the rotation of the earth and its position in relation to the sun, some parts of Alaska have 19+ hours of sunlight and almost no darkness during the summer months. So, for the first few days we were there, we didn't really sleep much. At 7 p.m., it still felt like it was 2 in the afternoon. We would leave to go fishing at 9 p.m. and stay out until 1 or 2 in the morning. It was great... at first.

But then the fatigue set in. After a few days of running on only a couple hours of sleep, we were starting to feel the effects. Our minds were becoming foggy, our eyes were blurry, and our heads were heavy. This phenomenon is known as "Midnight Sun", and there was only one solution - we needed darkness.

Just as the human body needs light in order to function properly, we need darkness just as much. In order for our minds and bodies to settle down and rest for a period of time, we need a tranquil, quiet, darkened space in which to retreat. Without it, we are destined to wander around in the middle of the night, trying to catch a fish or looking for an all-night diner. Trust me, it's not as fun as it sounds.

Does your bedroom have sufficient window coverings or blinds that help create a cocoon where your mind and body can recharge and rest? Can you purchase a bedside clock with a low light that won't be glaring in your face all through the night?

Make sleep a priority by powering down any electronic devices, such as phones, computers, and televisions, at least a full hour before you go to bed. Turn the lights down low a few hours before bedtime to let your brain know it's time to start winding down and relaxing. Cherish and protect your precious sleep by learning to embrace the darkness.

Ingredient #27:

Compassion

The other day I inadvertently replied to the wrong person in response to a text. As soon as I'd typed the message and hit send, I knew I had made a mistake. It wasn't anything to be worked up about or to be embarrassed by, just a simple mistake. But by the way I talked to myself after my minor goof, you'd have thought I had committed an unforgivable sin.

"Oh, my gosh! I am so stupid!" was my initial reaction. "Now that person is really going to think I'm an idiot! What is wrong with me?" Sound familiar? Why do we feel like it's okay to speak to or about ourselves in such a negative way? We would never talk to a friend, loved one, or even a stranger the way we talk to ourselves at times. Yet we all do it. For some of us, it is an almost constant, everyday occurrence. And we need to stop it.

Maybe it's human nature to berate ourselves, beat ourselves up, and criticize our own inadequacies. But that's no excuse. Yes, we are human. And that means that we are capable of growth. If we wish to send out love, tolerance, acceptance, and kindness into the world, it has to start with ourselves. We can and should practice compassion and forgiveness from within, opening up a place for understanding that starts in our own hearts and minds. We can silence the voice that points out every little thing we do wrong, and give voice to our wise inner self that knows that we are doing the best we can.

How do you talk to yourself? Do you call yourself names? Dwell on your imperfections? Use words like stupid, idiot, fat, lazy, or useless? Stop it. Right now. Start practicing compassion by giving yourself a break. No, you are not perfect. But neither is anyone else. You're a fantastic, amazing, loving, giving person. The next time you start to say bad things to or about yourself, remember that. You are human. You are imperfect. And you are enough. Just the way you are.

Ingredient #28:
Challenge

Last summer my husband and I decided to go on a day hike. We had heard people talking about a fairly easy-to-hike canyon in our area with a waterfall at the top. It sounded like a nice afternoon activity, so we grabbed our water bottles and a couple of snacks and off we went.

At first, the hike was nice and easy. The trail was well marked and sloped gently up the mountainside. There were lots of people on the trail that day, and the further up we climbed, the more climbers we noticed on their way down looking quite fatigued. Upon asking them, they informed us that they had turned around before they were able to reach to the top. We started to talk about possibly turning around, but some other hikers on the trail who had hiked the canyon before ensured us that we could make it. So we kept going.

After a few hours, I was starting to feel extremely fatigued. I wasn't sure I wanted to keep going. Maybe that waterfall at the top wasn't really worth the effort. The trail was getting rocky, my legs were burning, and my heart was pounding. Should I just give up? Just as I was clawing my way over a huge boulder, some hikers on their way down encouraged me. "You're almost there," they told me. "Keep going!" So I pushed through the pain and persevered.

Eventually, we made it to the top of the canyon, and stood in awe as we took in the view of the beautiful canyon and the massive waterfall. My lungs were burning, my head was throbbing, and I was a little light-headed. But I seriously felt great! Because I had pushed myself beyond what I thought I could do, I was rewarded with a feeling of accomplishment and pride. My body was capable of enduring more than I thought it could, and it was stronger than I usually gave it credit for.

How often do you give your body a chance to exceed your expectations? Give it a challenge. You may discover that your body is amazingly well equipped to handle much more than you think.

Ingredient #29:
Goals

We all know the importance of having goals in our lives. If we don't set goals for ourselves, we don't make much progress. The way we move from where we are to where we want to be is by setting goals. So maybe we have some goals for our physical bodies. Lose 20 pounds perhaps? Or get rid of that muffin top? Fit into those jeans? At first glance, those might seem like worthy aspirations. But what if we went just a tad deeper?

What if we moved beyond the initial impression of our bodies - what they look like to others, and what we see in the mirror? What if we started to think about how our bodies feel, move, rest, work and play? What if we gave our bodies love instead of hate, and compassion instead of punishment? Our goals for our bodies might be very different if we looked past the outward appearance, and took a look inside.

In my mid forties, I decided to set a goal - I wanted to be in the "best shape of my life" when I turned 50. I was a health coach, I had made huge changes and improvements in my life, and I felt confident that by the age of 50 I could really have it going on. Maybe even pose in a swimsuit showing off my flat abs, thin thighs, and slender hips. But eventually I realized that all I was doing was focusing on superficial, outward appearances that had very little to do with what "shape" my body was actually in. Looking good on the outside was a poor substitute for having tons of energy, getting good sleep, eating delicious food and loving my life.

I'll be turning 50 later on this year, and I honestly have no desire to pose for any pictures to document how healthy I am. I feel better than I have ever felt in my life. I'm at a healthy and reasonable weight. My spirituality is at an all-time high. I have great relationships with family and friends, and I'm genuinely happy. I've come to understand that being in the "best shape of my life" means I finally feel good in my own skin. It also means that I'm deeply grateful for this amazing gift I've been given, and I can honestly say that after years of self-hatred, I actually love myself. And I feel like that's a goal we can all work towards.

Ingredient #30:
Quiet

Sometimes I think that our external environment is a reflection of what's going on inside of us. Is your house always noisy, with people talking loudly, or maybe even arguing and yelling? Is the TV constantly blaring, even when the sofa is the only one around to watch it? Do you have a special playlist or radio station that must be playing in the background when you're driving? Does it bother you when you're required to stop talking for any length of time? Is it hard for you to listen, really listen, to others?

If our minds are noisy, chaotic, and restless, our outside world will be a mirror of that. Those of us who have a difficult time experiencing quiet should perhaps consider this question: Why is silence so hard for us? Don't get me wrong – I don't believe all noise is bad. In fact, some of it is absolutely wonderful.

When my three boys were growing up, our house was very rarely quiet. My oldest son played the trumpet, my middle son played the piano and drums, and my youngest played the cello. My two youngest were also singers, so there was always musical energy happening at our house in one way or another. And honestly, I loved it. I loved the sound of my boys expressing themselves through music. You never knew if someone was going to perform a Broadway musical at the dinner table, play the same song over and over again on the piano, or practice the cello late into the night. It was unpredictable and wonderful.

So, as our sons grew up and moved out one by one, our house grew more and more quiet. No more late-night serenades. No more trumpet practice. No more drum solos. It was hard at first. Really hard. They don't call it "Empty Nest Syndrome" for nothing. But I learned something in the quiet – I could be happy, truly happy, even without the noise.

I think we need silence as much as we need all the lovely sounds of life. In quiet moments, we can connect to our inner wisdom, ponder deeply, and access true peace. At some point in our lives, we will all experience silence. If we can learn to embrace it, we may discover that it's not quite as bad as we thought. We may even see it as a gift.

Ingredient #31:
Focus

In our society, multi-tasking has become the equivalent of competency. If you don't know how to multi-task, there must be something wrong with you. Only do one thing at a time? That's for babies. If you want to get ahead in life, get that promotion, reach all your goals and conquer the world, you'd better get your act together and start multi-tasking. If you don't, you'll be left behind.

I may be exaggerating just a little, but you get my point. I think women are especially vulnerable to falling into this trap. Because we take on many roles and responsibilities, we just assume that we should be able to do it all and then some, and all at the same time, no less! But there may be something to be said for focusing on one task, one problem, and one project at a time.

I'm a big fan of the TV show M.A.S.H., and I specifically remember a line from the character of Dr. Charles Emerson Winchester III. In the episode, some other doctors are trying to get him to work faster so he can save more patients. But he feels that if he tries to hurry or do too much, his work may suffer. His response: "I do one thing, I do it very well, and then, I move on."

What if we gave ourselves a break, and became a master of only one thing at a time? What if we did one thing very well, and then moved on to the next? What would that feel like? I'm thinking it would feel pretty freaking awesome! I know that when I have too many irons in the fire, I start to feel a pressure in my chest, like there's a burden pressing on me that I can't get out from underneath. If I run around all day without a precise plan, I rarely get much done.

Having a plan and bringing things into focus can help us feel less stressed and more accomplished. Write 3 prioritized lists in a planner or notebook; Must Do, Would Like To Do, and Would Love To Do. Then get to work on your lists. Do one thing. Do it very well. And then, move on. You'll find that having a plan and focusing on one task at a time will help you accomplish far more than trying to do it all at once.

Ingredient #32:

Acceptance

Have you ever met someone who absolutely despises having their picture taken? You know the kind – they turn away, run away, duck, or put their hand up to shield themselves from the camera as soon as they notice it pointing in their direction. Have YOU ever been that person? I know I have. Sometimes I feel that the prospect of having an imperfect image of myself captured for all time on film, video, or social media is excruciatingly unbearable. I'd almost rather go to the dentist and have a tooth pulled than endure the agony of posing for a simple photograph.

But I didn't always shy away from the camera. When I was a little girl at my older sibling's wedding, the photographer took a picture of me at the refreshment table. I was sipping punch out of a glass cup with my pinky finger raised and, with all due credit to a great photographer and timing, my eyes were sparkling beyond belief. It was a great picture, I must admit. The photographer liked it so much he even hung a giant print of it in the front window of his shop on Main Street. Needless to say, I loved the attention and for a while I thought I was some kind of mini celebrity. I showed that photo to anyone and everyone who came to our home for the next ten years.

So how did I go from a child who proudly showed off her photo to anyone and everyone to an adult who trembles at the mere mention of the word "camera"? I think it may have something to do with a lack of acceptance. As children, we have no filters and no shame. Those come later – usually after years of being told that we have to be quiet, behave ourselves, and settle down. Little by little, we retreat into ourselves, and become less accepting of our true natures. We begin to feel that we have to hide those aspects of ourselves that others may find annoying, distracting, or hard to put up with. And before we know it, we are criticizing and finding fault with all aspects of ourselves.

What if we returned to our carefree, non-judgmental natures? What if we opened up our hearts and loved and accepted everyone exactly as they are? And what if we started with ourselves? Try opening up, smiling for the camera, and letting your light shine. You may just find yourself feeling like a mini celebrity.

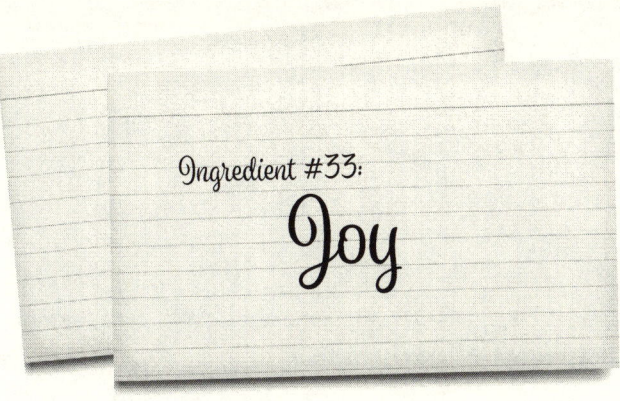

Ingredient #33:
Joy

I love music. And I love listening to music while driving my car. But I must clarify something – I don't just listen, because that would be mind-numbingly boring for me. I have to sing along. Loudly. Sometimes obnoxiously. But there's a reason I do this – because singing brings me joy.

I can think of several occasions where I have been in my car, sitting at a stoplight, singing away and thoroughly enjoying myself. Then the person in the car next to me sees me. Busted! Do I get embarrassed? Yep. Do I stop singing? Absolutely not. I might tone it down a little until traffic starts moving again, but I just don't seem to be able to stop myself. And I'm not sure I want to.

Something else that brings me joy is my family. I love being with them, and I spend as much time as I can in their company. If I can't physically be near them, I call them on the phone. I stay connected to them because if I didn't, my life would be pretty darn sad. They are my biggest source of joy in life, and I can't imagine where I would be without them.

I believe we were put on this planet to experience joy. Not just a fleeting moment of happiness or satisfaction every now and then, but a continual stream of the kind of joy you feel deep in your bones. Being alive is an amazing thing. Think about all of the intricate, complex functions of your body, and all it does for you every moment of every day. It's amazing! Just being alive in this moment is a cause for celebration!

Living and breathing joy is our birthright. And if we don't claim it, we only have ourselves to blame. So do what brings you joy, whether it's singing in the car, dancing in the rain, basking in the sun, or running through the sprinklers. Life is way, way too short to go around feeling gloomy and sour. Decide what makes you the happiest, and then pursue it relentlessly. Don't wait for someone or something outside of yourself to bring it to you. Forget about what it might look like to anyone else, and just embrace the joy of living.

Ingredient #34:
Purpose

What is your purpose in life? This is a question that has haunted mankind since the beginning of time. To know your purpose, to have a sense of why you were put here on this earth seems to be the ultimate holy grail – it's something we all search for but rarely, if ever, find. But what if having a purpose isn't as complicated as we think it is? What if we all have a common purpose in life? What if knowing our purpose is as easy as simply taking a breath?

There was a time when I believed that my purpose in life was to be a mother. I was blessed with three wonderful sons who mean the world to me, and for many years caring for them and tending to their needs consumed the majority of my waking hours. Bathing, feeding, loving, and raising children is a full-time job with no pay, little rest, and zero sick leave. The benefits, however, are unsurpassed by any other occupation or pursuit. Mothering is most assuredly a labor of love, and, as all parents can attest, a most rewarding and satisfying effort. But was motherhood really my only purpose?

Once my days were no longer filled with diapers, homework, carpools, and soccer practice, I began to search for a new means of bringing purpose to my life. I felt that I needed to continue on the path of nurturing, caring for, and supporting others. I began a career as a health coach, writer, and healer, which offered once again that feeling of satisfaction, and yes, a sense of purpose. I truly love writing, and I am passionate about helping others heal through my coaching and speaking. But is being a healer the only reason for my existence?

We are all here as a result of one thing: love. Our spirits and bodies were created out of love, and our purpose has everything to do with that powerful force. Can we learn to love, even in less than ideal circumstances, surrounded by less than perfect people? Can we give, receive, perpetuate, and exude love, even in an atmosphere of pain, grief, and suffering? If we can, then we have found our purpose. The purpose and meaning of life for each and every one of us is to love. No conditions. No exceptions. Just love. It's simple, but also deeply profound. If you have learned to love, then you have learned your purpose.

Ingredient #35:

Awe

Have you ever been driving down the road and suddenly noticed a magnificent sunset? Or perhaps you've noticed the crickets chirping outside your window in the evening, and it was as if you were hearing that soothing sound for the very first time. There are moments in life that can take our breath away, and most of the time they appear out of nowhere. These are the magical moments when we realize how beautiful, fragile, and amazing life truly is. These are the moments of awe that our bodies, minds and souls crave.

I love getting up early every morning for what I call my "Sacred Time". This is my time to read, meditate, journal, pray, and connect to my inner wisdom and higher power. If something happens and I miss my Sacred Time, I feel deprived and slightly annoyed that I was denied that time for myself. It has become a part of my day that is essential, even crucial, to my health and wellbeing.

My Sacred Time starts with gratitude. Being grateful, and feeling that gratitude deep in our bones, is a powerful practice and a great way to start off a new day. Not sure what you have to feel thankful for? Open your eyes. Do you have a bed to sleep in? Say thank you. Do you have nice clothes to wear? Say thank you. Do you have a job to go to? Say thank you. Do you have someone to love? Say thank you. There is always, always, always something to be grateful for. All we need to do is look around us.

It's true that life gives us little moments of awe now and then, and without a doubt we should appreciate them when they come. But it is also on us to create our own moments – to make space in our day to say thank you to the Universe. When we do, we experience the childlike wonder of being alive, right now, in this exact moment. It's humbling. And powerful.

Get in the habit of feeling deep gratitude for the many gifts and blessings you've been given. Create a "Wow" moment right now by stopping to reflect on just how incredible life can be. And don't forget to say, "Thank you."

Ingredient #36:
Gentleness

We tend to be a society of extremes. If you don't believe me, just look at the titles of some of the more popular television shows we love to watch - programs like "Survivor", "The Biggest Loser", and "Man vs. Wild" come to mind. Great emphasis seems to be placed on pushing our limits, keeping things intense, and experiencing a more stunning transformation than our competitors. I suppose it makes for great entertainment, but how realistic is it to always be pushing further, harder and faster? After a while, it's just plain exhausting.

While it's true that our bodies do crave some hard-core, gut-busting, sweat-inducing activities once in a while, they also crave something else - gentleness. Ideally, as babies, we were gently cradled in our parents' arms, rocked soothingly, and spoken to in hushed voices. It's instinctual to be gentle with newborns, because they are so tiny, helpless, and fragile. As adults, we naturally still crave that gentle treatment from time to time, and most often it falls upon us to provide that nurturing for ourselves.

Now, it's not practical for a full-grown adult to expect to be rocked, cradled, or sung a lullaby. That would just be weird. But it's not that unreasonable to think that we can be gentle with ourselves, and to give our bodies some nurturing and comfort every now and then. Instead of an extreme makeover, how does some extreme self-care sound?

Would you find it relaxing to take a long soak in a hot bubble bath at the end of a stressful day? If so, make sure to set aside some time a few nights a week just for such an indulgence. Maybe you would love to light some candles, pour a cup of tea, and kick back with a good book for an hour or two. If that sounds good to you, then by all means do it. And don't feel guilty! Honestly, you really do deserve it.

Instead of pushing ourselves to the limit and becoming physically, mentally and emotionally exhausted, let's try a little tenderness. Let's be gentle with ourselves, and maybe, if we're lucky, it will help us be gentler with each other as well.

Ingredient #37:
Color

The other day I was visiting a friend at her house, and I was uplifted and inspired by the way her home was decorated. There were sunny orange pillows on the soft-grey sofa, bright purple flowers in a vase on the table, and cheerful, multi-colored paintings on the walls. Her home felt happy, vibrant, and welcoming, and my friend had a personality to match. There's something about color that just brings everything and everyone to life.

Contrast that with another home I visited recently: Old shaggy, brown carpeting that had seen better days, dark colored walls, and a plain, tan, and rather worn-out looking sofa. The vibe in the first home seemed to say, "Welcome home! We're so glad you're here!", while the feel of the second home was more like, "Go away!"

Don't get me wrong – I'm not saying you need to go out and buy all new furniture and decor for your house (unless you want to). But if, like the second home I described, yours is a little drab and dull, perhaps you could add a colorful throw blanket or a vase of fresh flowers. You'd be surprised

73

how much it lifts your spirits to have a beautiful floral arrangement in your kitchen window for a few days. Maybe you could give an old dresser a fresh coat of paint, or throw a new funky rug down on the entryway floor.

Besides brightening up your home, there are lots of other ways you can bring more color into your life. Spice up your wardrobe with a hot pink blouse or a bright red necklace. If you're feeling bold, buy a new pair of shoes in a color you've never dared wear before. Plant some yellow day lilies in your yard, or some strawberries on your back deck. Throw some fresh blueberries and raspberries on your oatmeal in the morning, or some lovely, dark-green kale in your scrambled eggs.

Color is important. Color is life! We only need to step outside and look at what Mother Nature has created for us to see that. From the flowers and the rainbows to the birds and the trees, all of nature is colorful, vibrant, pulsating, and alive. Our bodies and minds need the variety and interest of color in order to feel their very best. See if you can find a way to add color to your life - it's what Nature intended.

Ingredient #38:
Irreverence

Most comedians make their living from taking a common human experience and giving it an irreverent twist. It catches us off guard. It even shocks us a little. And we laugh, sometimes until tears are streaming down our cheeks. The same can be said for profanity – when we hear a "bad word", we are usually caught off guard, a little shocked, and more often than not, we chuckle. Honestly, I think most of us could benefit from a little coarse language now and then. You may disagree with me on this, but before you slam this book shut, just hear me out.

Historically, swear words can be linked back to taboo subjects - things people were uncomfortable talking about. Sex, excrement, and religion are just a few. So when folks used profanity, they were bringing out into the open the off-limits topics that no one wanted to discuss. Even today, swearing demystifies and humanizes what we're all thinking but may be too afraid to say out loud.

Cussing can also help alleviate emotional and physical pain. One study even found that test subjects could hold their hand in a bucket of ice water longer if they said "shit" rather than "shoot." I have personally found this to be true. I recently broke my toe, and rather than break down in tears, I chose to cuss like a sailor for a minute or two. I may have shocked my husband a bit, but I didn't cry, and I think the swearing really did help ease my pain.

Some of the best books I've read have profane words in the title. "Do Cool Sh*t" by Miki Agrawal, "You Are A Bada**" by Jen Sincero, and "F*ck That: An Honest Meditation" by Jason Headley are all books that I would recommend to friends and even give as gifts. To me, the names of these books imply that maybe we need to lighten up a little and not take life quite so seriously. Cussing is irreverent and playful, and unlike in the middle ages, when swear words were believed to literally ascend to heaven and injure God himself, it's pretty harmless.

Obviously we don't want to offend children or be discriminatory in any way, and we must watch the timing and frequency of our vulgarity. But if a little cuss word escapes your lips every now and then, don't sweat it. You're only human. And nobody gives a shit anyway.

Ingredient #39:
Fresh Air

Now that it's summer in my part of the world, my favorite thing to do is to take my little laptop and move my office outside for the day. After many long months of winter and a very long, wet, spring, I am more than ready to spend some time in the great outdoors! It's as if my body is saying to me, "Let me out of these four walls! I need some fresh air, pronto!"

Most of us spend the majority of our lives indoors. Unless our line of work requires us to be outside, we are indoors for at least 8 hours during the workday and 8 to 10 hours while we sleep, eat, prepare for bed, etc. That leaves very little time to spend with Mother Nature. But it's Mother Nature, not our cubicle, that calls out to us and begs us to come and play. Our lungs are eager to inhale and exhale deeply. Our ears crave the sound of trees rustling and birds singing. Our eyes long for a glimpse of a freshly blooming flower. Our skin yearns for the warmth and glow of the sun.

It makes sense to me that our bodies want and even demand time in a natural environment. Indoors we are exposed to fluorescent lighting, electrical appliances, dusty, re-circulated air, and stagnant, lingering smells. Outside we are surrounded by oxygen producing plants, trees, and creatures that are alive and moving and growing. Life is happening just outside our door! No wonder we feel more alive and vibrant when we step outside for some fresh air and sunshine!

One of my favorite places to visit is New York City. Even with all of its tall buildings, subways, traffic and tourists, New York has a special haven – Central Park. Here city dwellers can sit on the grass, feed the ducks, ride a bike, or take a leisurely stroll. I think it's incredible that whoever planned out this amazing city made sure to save plenty of room for its citizens to get out and commune with nature!

Make getting fresh air a priority in your daily life. If only for a few minutes a day, but preferably longer, get outside, inhale deeply, and connect with the world around you. Take it all in. Enjoy the sights, sounds and textures of the earth. And just breathe.

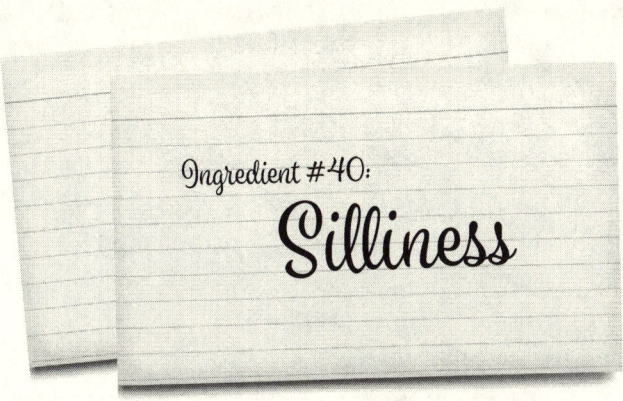

Ingredient #40:
Silliness

A horse walks into a bar, and the bartender says, "Why the long face?"

A toothless termite walks into a bar and asks, "Is the bar tender here?"

What did the duck say when she bought a new lipstick? "Put it on my bill."

A man got hit in the head with a diet cola. He's okay though – it was a soft drink.

Okay, so maybe these jokes aren't exactly knee-slappers, but they're pretty silly. And a little bit of silliness goes a long way in making our lives more enjoyable. What silly thing have you done lately? When was the last time you did the chicken dance, the hokey pokey, or walked like an Egyptian? How often do you treat your friends and family to an impromptu karaoke performance of your favorite song or your best Elvis impersonation?

Some of the happiest memories I have are of times when people were being totally silly. Like the time my husband and I somehow ended up in a dance contest at a restaurant/bar in Mexico. First prize was a bottle of tequila, and we don't even drink! Or that time my sister and I took selfies on her phone and laughed until we cried. It probably wasn't funny to anyone else, but we thought it was hilarious.

I think the reason these wacky moments are so enjoyable has to do with the fact that, for a few minutes, we're not stressing about the past or worrying about the future, we're just fully present in the here and now. Silliness gets us out of our heads and into our hearts, where we are free to express our thoughts and emotions without fear of judgment.

Why not take some time to be silly today? Tell a not-so-funny joke, sing off-key, and dance like nobody's watching. Or you could play it safe and just act normal. But that would just be silly.

Ingredient #41:
Faith

Today I'm reflecting on the horrible tragedies that been inflicted on innocent people by those who claim to do so because of their faith or religious beliefs. Mass shootings. Café bombings. Train derailments. Hijacking and crashing of airplanes. These acts of terrorism are only about one thing: violence. They have absolutely nothing to do with faith. Faith in no way, shape or form caused these events to occur, but it is faith that will see us through them and where we will ultimately find peace.

During times of personal, community, or national grief, when we struggle to understand the why of a senseless or vicious attack, we need something to hold onto. We need to believe that, at the end of the day, something beautiful will emerge from the pain, that good will eventually defeat evil, and that love will ultimately triumph over hate. That's where faith comes in.

Where reason fails to comfort and logic falls short, faith comes in and saves the day. Faith assures us that the sun will rise again tomorrow, and we will bask in the light once again. Faith picks us up from our crumpled heap of sorrow, kisses us on the forehead, and gently strokes our hair. Faith stands by our side while we scream and sob and cry out for revenge, then she simply takes us by the hand and leads us to a place where we can rest.

There may be times when we feel like we have lost faith, but she never completely leaves us, even in the darkest hours. Even when we are so numb that we can barely move, or so angry that we feel that at any second we might explode, or so grief-stricken that we fear our hearts may shatter into a million pieces, faith is there. In a quiet moment, she slides in next to us, embraces us, and warms us with her light.

Whether we attach it to a power greater than ourselves or simply to the assurance of a brighter day ahead, faith helps us resist the urge to close off and shut down. It is only when we allow faith full and unlimited access to our hearts that she can lift us from our ashes and carry us toward a better tomorrow.

Ingredient #42:

Touch

If you've ever treated yourself to a professional massage, you know the importance and power of touch. If you've ever received a warm embrace from a long-absent friend or loved one, you know the healing and comfort that comes from human contact. Touch is one of the key components of our existence. It is one of the five senses that allow us to experience all the sensations and wonders of being alive. And yet, so often, we forget to utilize this incredible power in our interactions with others.

When a baby is born, one of the first things the nurse or midwife will do is lay the newborn on the mother's chest. This skin-to-skin contact is crucial to the health of the infant and marks the beginning of the bonding process between mother and child. If this contact doesn't occur, the baby fails to thrive and develop normally. We, as human beings, simply cannot survive without intimate human contact. But in our modern society, it has become all too easy to live without much human interaction at all. Internet chat rooms and telecommuting have become the new normal, replacing face-to-face meetings and conversations around the water cooler.

Living in an electronic age has made it possible for us to connect with people all over the world, and that's an incredible thing. But I think we have to be careful that we don't become so immersed in our virtual world that we miss out on connecting with those who are right here in front of us. Clicking a "like" or "love" button is a great way to support a friend, but in most cases it's far more effective to reach out a hand or give a hug or a kiss. Nothing will ever be able to fully replace the loving touch of one person to another.

How can you get more in "touch" with those closest to you? Can you go to dinner with your family and make eye contact with them rather than with your phone messages? Can you give a friend a hug that lasts longer than three Mississippis? When you make a new acquaintance, can you shake with both hands, not just one? If you make the effort to put your arm around a few more shoulders, hug a few more strangers, and squeeze a few more hands, I promise you, no one will be mad about it.

Ingredient #43:
Simplicity

Why does it seem to be so complicated to simplify our lives? Simplicity implies that things will become less complicated once we simplify them, but the process of simplifying can be anything but simple. Did that even make sense? Let me simplify it a little.

Say you have a goal to spend less time shopping for groceries, clothing, and other life essentials. You would like to spend less time running around like a crazy person and more time relaxing and enjoying life, but you love a bargain. So what can you do? You can get an app that stores all of your card information, punch cards and coupons to simplify the shopping process. But first you have to locate all of the cards, input all the data into the app, and create passwords and usernames for each account. Not so simple.

Or let's say you set an intention to keep your home more organized and less cluttered, but how do you go about it? If you're like me, you buy several books about how to get more organized, take a few online courses on organization, then finally, you go through and purge your closets, cupboards, and storage room. Now you have a giant pile of stuff that you either need to donate to charity, give away to friends and relatives, or sell on eBay. Nothing simple about that.

If the definition of simplify is to make things easier, we are clearly missing the mark. When I think of true simplicity, I think of my grandmother. She lived a rich, interesting life filled with creativity, service, and sacrifice. Her modest home was neat and welcoming, but not extravagant. She had maybe five dresses hanging in her closet. Her small jewelry box contained a few brooches, a watch, and two or three beaded necklaces. She never learned how to drive a car, and never traveled very far from her home. But she was happy with her lifestyle, and I never once heard her complain or wish for more.

If we can be content with what we have, and realize that what we have is all we need, I think we will end up being happier too. It's great to get organized and purge once in a while, but our real focus should be on how we can be happy here and now, with exactly what we have. It's just that simple.

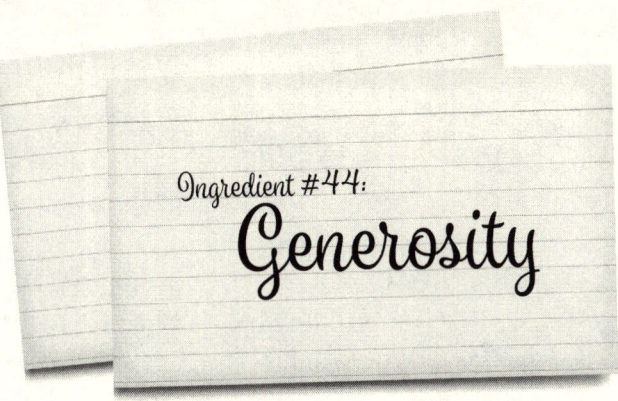

Ingredient #44:
Generosity

When was the last time you gave until it hurt? How long has it been since someone protested because what you were giving was much too generous? If it's been a while, maybe it would be helpful to check in with your heart and ask what is holding you back from giving freely and liberally.

I have a wonderful friend whom I have known since we were four years old. We haven't always kept in close contact over the years, but whenever we get to see each other it's as if not a day has passed. Those kinds of friends are extremely rare – the kind you hang on to no matter what. Recently, I was giving a talk at a local author's event and posted an invitation on social media for friends to come by if they had time and were in the area. My amazing childhood friend drove 4 ½ hours to surprise me and attend my big night! I can't even explain how much it meant to me to have my sweet friend make such an effort in my behalf.

Being generous has nothing to do with how much extra stuff you have lying around or how big your bank account is. Generosity comes from the heart. It took zero dollars for my friend to show up at an event that she knew was very important to me, except for maybe what it cost her in gas. What it did take was time out of her busy schedule and away from her family, which is even more precious if you ask me. But her generous spirit and her love for me were stronger than her desire to be comfortable. Yes, being generous sometimes means being uncomfortable. That's why it isn't always easy.

As good as it feels to be on the receiving end of someone else's generosity, it feels even better to be the one doing the giving. Our hearts crave that feeling of giving up something we treasure in order to lift and support someone else. Instead of looking out for #1, practice looking out for a friend. Instead of trying to get the best end of the deal, try being overly generous. You may discover that giving until it hurts is one of the best feelings in the world.

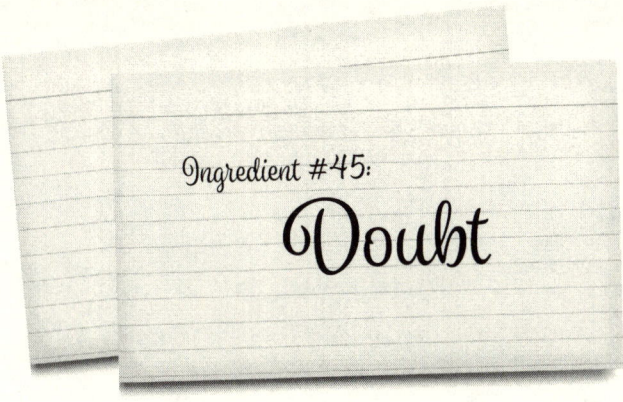

Ingredient #45:

Doubt

Have you ever had a conversation with someone who seems to have all the answers? They know why the sky is blue, why the grass is green, and how that tiny ship ended up in that glass bottle. I'm not saying it's a bad thing to possess knowledge and understand how things work. I think we should all pursue knowledge every single day of our lives. But sometimes, without even realizing it, we get caught up in all that we know, and we forget that there is so much we don't know, so much we will never fully understand, and some things that will forever make us scratch our heads and wonder, maybe even doubt.

But is doubt such a bad thing? I don't think it is. When we are in doubt, it means we are in a place where we can learn. To doubt is to acknowledge that some information is missing, or unseen at this moment, and more investigating and learning is needed. Doubt can move us from a rigid and uncompromising way of thinking to a more flexible, open state of mind. If we let it, doubt can be a wonderful teacher, a remarkable gift, and a catalyst for incredible change.

There was a time in my life (yes, when I was younger) that I thought I had all the answers. I had my life planned out, and I was certain about what the future held in store for me. Lucky for me, the universe had a different idea and my life turned out how it was supposed to, not how I thought it would or how I had once wanted it to. I can see that now, but at the time, I was devastated. I began to have doubts. I started to wonder if I had been dead wrong all along. And that's when I was really able to start learning. Life was teaching me the lessons I needed to learn in ways I would never have dreamed of or even thought possible. I'm thankful for that season of doubt, because without it I would have been a hollowed-out version of myself.

What are you absolutely sure of? Try giving yourself permission to question it, to explore other possibilities, to doubt. You may find that letting go of certainty is a doorway to learning and growth. It may make you uncomfortable, it might be a little scary, but will it be worth it? No doubt about it.

Ingredient #46:
Community

Have you ever been at a party, surrounded by people on all sides, yet felt totally alone? Or maybe you've been on a crowded bus or subway, pressed up so close to other humans you can tell what they ate for lunch, and yet you still felt isolated, even lonely. I think we have all experienced this at least once in our lives, and it's probably not a feeling we would deliberately choose to experience again. So how is it that we can feel so alone, so disconnected, even in a crowd? It's all about a feeling of community.

Most of us have our "people", our tribe - a group that we identify with and with whom we share common interests or beliefs. Our community could be a family, a group of friends, a book club, a sports team, a religious congregation, or a political party. No matter what type of organization or club we belong to, the key is that we *belong*. We fit. We are a part of something larger than ourselves.

If something happens that severs our ties to our community, it can cause feelings of anxiety, depression, and despair. We may go in search of another faction to replace the one we have lost. Or we might start our own new and improved group to fill the void. Our need to belong is in our DNA. We are programmed to find safety and security within a group. It's how we have survived throughout history.

Coming together within a community gives our lives purpose, direction, and meaning. That is not to say that we will always agree 100% with every value, every tradition, and every rule of a group with which we associate, and nor should we. Each one of us has a unique perspective, something only we can contribute. Ideally, we should be willing and able to express our personal views as well as be open to the ideas and thoughts of others within the group. If this is not the case, it may be time to move on to a different community or form a new one.

Studies show that a sense of belonging improves our health and happiness and increases feelings of motivation and persistence. So whether you're a member of the Bar association or you just hang out at a local bar, check in with your peeps every now and then and renew those ties. I promise you won't regret it.

Ingredient #47:
Feelings

Shame. Despair. Regret. Sorrow. Agony. Fear. Heartache. Some of the worst moments we experience in life can be described with these words. They are all feelings - emotions that make us wish we could just disappear into nothingness in order to escape the torture. Emotions can overwhelm us, consume us, and weigh us down. But there are also moments of love, connection, joy, bliss, contentment, and peace. When we experience these feelings, we wish that life could last forever so we could always feel what we're feeling in that wonderful moment in time. As humans, we're meant to experience both ends of the emotional spectrum – the lowest of lows and highest of highs – as well as everything in between.

It may be that we, or others in our lives, view having a wide range of emotional experiences as abnormal, undesirable, or even dangerous. Perhaps the idea that life should be calm and steady at all times is just too appealing to resist. Or maybe the highs and lows of life are too overwhelming, too complicated, or too much for some of us to handle. Many times - too many, in fact - we medicate ourselves in order to get off the roller coaster of emotions. Whether it is with food, alcohol, sex, illegal drugs, or prescribed medications, we numb ourselves to the point of not feeling anything. And when we do, life becomes flat - bearable, but flat nonetheless.

How often do we turn on the TV and tune out our family members in order to avoid discussion or conflict? How many of us seek solace in a shopping mall or browsing online rather than openly and honestly communicating with our friends and loved ones? Feelings are hard, and consequently, much of the time we simply don't deal with them. We shut down, we avoid, we disconnect.

Feelings make life complicated and messy, but I'm pretty sure that's exactly how it's supposed be. On this crazy, scary, and sometimes nauseating ride, we may hit some unexpected curves, experience whiplash, and be thrown for a loop. It's insane. But trying to live up to unrealistic ideas of what your life should be is the true definition of insanity. You were created to feel, and there's absolutely no shame in that.

Ingredient #48:
Mindfulness

When was the last time you paused for a few moments and just sat quietly? I mean actually just sat there, not looking at your phone or thumbing through a magazine or browsing the internet or dozing off. Never? If that's the case, don't feel too bad, because you're not alone. The majority of us don't make a habit of being still. Frankly, most of us barely have time during the day to simply take a deep breath, let alone set aside time for meditation. In fact, I know people who are so busy that they have to schedule in bathroom breaks or they won't even have time for that! But the more I learn about and practice the art of mindfulness, the more I realize how important to our health and well-being it really is.

I recently began taking a few minutes each day to just sit, be still, breathe in and out, and listen to my inner wisdom. I'll admit, it wasn't easy at first. No sooner than I began would my mind proceed to find reasons to rebel against my quest for serenity. Negative thoughts would pop into my head, that incessant voice would start chattering away, and my body would begin to feel the stress. "How long is this going to take? Has it even been five minutes yet? I have so much to get done today, I should really get my butt in gear. This is stupid. What if someone walked in and saw me just sitting here, doing nothing? How crazy would that look?"

Even with that initial resistance, I persevered, determined to find out if all of the hype about meditation was actually true. And what I discovered was that, though it didn't happen immediately, I did begin to feel more centered and calm on the days I practiced being mindful. When stressful events happened during the day, I was able to remain focused and alert to what needed to be done. It was almost as if taking a few minutes each morning to check in with myself gave me a sense of competence and awareness that hadn't been there before.

A simple meditation to start with is the Buddhist tradition of conscious breathing. *"Breathing in, I calm my body. Breathing out, I smile. Dwelling in the present moment, I know this is a wonderful moment."* Give mindfulness a try. You may find that even a few minutes of practice each day can bring about big changes in your body, mind, and spirit.

Ingredient #49:
Grace

I spent the first 30 or more years of my life trying - I mean trying *really* hard - to earn my place in this world. I thought that if I tried my hardest, worked the longest, and squeezed every ounce of effort out of myself, then, and only then, I would be worthy. I would be enough. Worthy of what, you ask? Enough of what? I didn't know. I just thought I had to try. So I tried and I tried and I tried. But no matter how hard I tried, I always felt like I fell short. I needed to *do* more. I needed to try harder. My focus was always on what *I* could do. What *I* had to give. But one day, in the not too distant past, I realized something – it was never about me.

During my sacred morning time, I often study topics that interest me or that I feel compelled to learn more about. I recently became aware that, although I had always heard the term "grace", I didn't really understand it or know how it worked. So I began to research and study the topic of grace. And the more I studied and learned, the more I came to realize that grace could not be earned. With all of my striving and doing and trying, I could never "earn" my way into God's or the Universe's good grace, because, well, I was already there. Grace is a gift that is given freely and unconditionally, no strings attached. There's nothing we can do to earn it, no merit badge to qualify for, no star on the forehead of the over-achiever. All we need to do to receive grace is accept it. That's it.

Grace is release. Grace is acceptance. Grace is an acknowledgement that we are not in control. Grace is resting in the assurance that everything is and will be okay, even if we can't see it right now. Grace is knowing that God or the Universe or your higher power has your back, and you don't have to keep struggling, fighting, and pushing. Grace is gratitude for the knowledge that our efforts don't have to be perfect. That we don't have to be perfect.

Maybe it's time to stop trying so hard and just relax into grace. When we accept and live in grace, our efforts no longer come from a place of urgency and stress, but from a place of peace and assurance. We do our best. We are loving and kind. And we know that wherever we fall short, grace will more than make up the difference.

Ingredient #50:
Grace

Did you know that our bodies are constantly changing and regenerating themselves at any given moment? For example, the cells that line the inside of your stomach and intestines are replaced every few days. Your skin cells slough off and are replaced pretty much on a daily basis. And some highly specialized white blood cells only last a few hours before being replaced. Change is literally in our DNA – we are never exactly the same from one moment to the next. Change is a natural process of life, and yet we tend to resist it. Why? I think it's because change can be scary and uncomfortable. There's a part of us that wants everything to remain the same simply because it feeds the illusion that we are in control.

But there's another part of us, the wiser part, I think, that craves change. The reassurance and familiarity of sameness actually pales in comparison to the excitement and rush of newness. Every morning, when we awaken, it's as if we have been reborn. The dawning of a new day holds the promise of fresh adventures and unexplored possibilities. It's almost as if the old self dies with the darkness, and a new self is created with the light. Without this constant flow of changing energy, this continual movement of creativity, we would literally die. Life means growth, regeneration, progress, and transformation. Isn't it incredible that each and every morning we get to be reminded of this miraculous process?

Nature is a wise teacher, and we need to look no further than the grass, trees, and flowers to learn a lesson about change. The grass grows, each blade reaching toward the sun until it is mowed down, only to begin growing again immediately. A tree starts out as a tiny seed, but within that seed lives the possibility of a great oak. Flowers burst through the soil as tiny green buds, eventually transforming into beautiful, colorful blossoms. All of life is buzzing and vibrating, constantly in a state of flux and growth. Why should we think we are any different?

Give yourself permission today to let go of any fears you may have surrounding change. Let each breath you take be joyful - feel the renewal of life that comes with every precious beat of your heart. Embrace change. Embrace impermanence. And embrace peace.

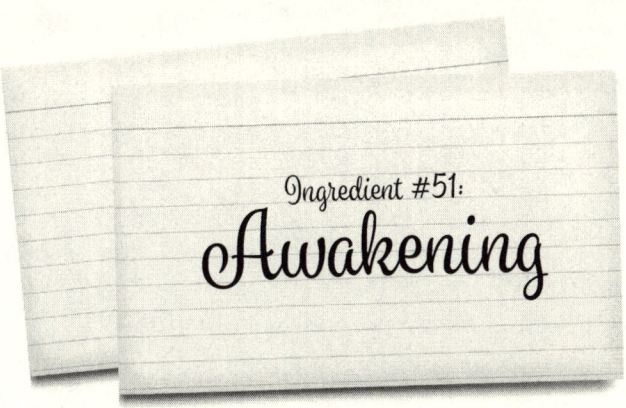

Ingredient #51:
Awakening

Throughout history, mankind has been in the process of awakening. From the Stone Age and the Dark Ages to the Renaissance and the Age of Enlightenment, we have been on a journey of illumination. It is a time-proven fact that men and women have the capacity to evolve, improve, and increase in wisdom and understanding. We no longer live in caves and forage for our food in the wilderness, nor do we continue to believe that the world is flat or that the sun revolves around the earth. We have awakened to a higher knowledge than we had at the time that those events were occurring.

It would be foolish and perhaps even irresponsible to believe that we are done evolving, or that our understanding has reached its climax and there is no more work that needs to be done. The human race still has many complex issues to tackle, and societies worldwide remain in need of enlightenment regarding the basic human rights of those who don't fall within the "norms" of those societies. Women are still oppressed, people of different races or ethnicity continue to be discriminated against, children are still abused, and gay, lesbian, and transgender people are still marginalized and shamed. Although as a human race we have come a long way, we still have a long way to go.

What is our part in all of this? How can we contribute to the evolution of the collective consciousness and thus ensure the hope for a brighter future for our children and grandchildren? If we are not at the forefront of scientific discovery or leading the way in the human rights movements, is there anything we can do to contribute? I believe there is.

Awakening begins with one person – just one – who is willing to see things in a new light. We can open our minds to the possibility of an idea we may not have considered a few years, months, or even moments before. We can let go of ego, self-centeredness, and the need to be right in favor of love, unity, acceptance, and peace. We can actively seek out enlightenment rather than waiting for it to find us. Awakening is not only possible, it's inevitable. And all we need to do is give it a chance to take root in our hearts.

Ingredient #52:
Love

We end where we began, with love, because I believe that love is the basis for all healing and growth. I can't emphasize this enough: love is the most crucial ingredient of all! Love and respect for our bodies and for our "selves" forms the foundation for physical, emotional, and spiritual health. Love and compassion for others is the starting point for healing our relationships, our communities, our nations, and our world. Love is the greatest force in the universe, and if we let it, it can transform us into more than we ever imagined possible.

Love transforms a fist full of dandelions gathered by a child into a beautiful bouquet of roses in the eyes of a mother. Love creates a magnificent palace out of the humble, sparsely furnished apartment of a newly married couple. Love can bring the hope of sunshine to a gloomy day and the promise of a brighter tomorrow to the darkest night. Love turns the ordinary into the extraordinary.

Like I said at the beginning of this book, the ingredient we all need more of is love. In order to receive love, we need to give it, and we absolutely need to start with ourselves. If being critical of yourself is how you usually roll, that ends today. Here are some ways in which you can begin:

From now on, only speak kindly to and about yourself. Make a new rule that negativity, criticism, and faultfinding is not allowed.

Say "I love you" out loud while looking in the mirror.

Write "I love you" on your hand.

Write yourself a note of encouragement.

Practice being grateful for each and every aspect of your body and all it does for you every day.

Do whatever it takes to learn to love yourself. Your life literally depends on it.

After you love yourself, you can then begin to love others. Here's how:

Generously compliment strangers, family members, and friends. Never leave a kind word unspoken.

Give the gift of time – time to listen, time to share, and time to just be.

Say, "I love you" like you mean it, because you do!

Forgive freely.

Ask for forgiveness quickly.

Apologize sincerely.

Talk openly and honestly.

Do this right now: close your eyes and visualize your heart as an open conduit of love and light that never closes. As you inhale, imagine love as a soft, pink light, flowing in and filling your body and soul until it is over-flowing. As you exhale, visualize this flow of love and light emanating from you and cascading over everyone you meet. You can use this visualization anytime you feel the need for more love or support in your life.

Let love transform you. Let it heal you. And then go out and heal the world.